老子
LAO TZU

(c.571 BC-471 BC)

The Wisdom of China

LAO TZU
The Eternal Tao Te Ching

By Xu Yuanxiang & Yin Yongjian

CHINA INTERCONTINENTAL PRESS

CONTENTS

Introduction / *9*

Lao Tzu and Taoism / *15*

Story of Lao Tzu / *25*

Lao Tzu in History Books / *37*

Lao Tzu and Chinese Culture / *65*

Lao Tzu's Theory of Government / *81*

Influence on the World / *97*

Tao Te Ching / *105*

Famous Sayings from 'Tao Te Ching' / *115*

微之必固興之將欲奪之必固興之是謂微弱勝剛強魚不可脫於淵國之利器不可示人道常無為而無不為侯王若能守之萬物將自化化而欲作吾將鎮之以無名之樸亦將不欲不欲以靜天下將自正上德不德是以有德下德不失德是以無德無為而無以為下德為之而有以為上

Introduction

In a rural area in the northern part of China, a wedding is taking place. The ritual is a strange but revealing mixture of Eastern and Western traditions and cultures; of the modern and the ancient. The groom and the bride wear Western-style dress, not the traditional long gown or cheongsam. However, many of the rituals still observed in Chinese weddings date back thousands of years and are a living echo of ancient Chinese teachings. The bride and groom still make traditional obeisances to their parents and each other as well as to the Heavens and the Earth. Thus, some 20 percent of the world's population still honor traditions and customs that date back over two millennia. When Christians

Bowing to the Heavens and the Earth is a traditional Chinese custom.

marry, they commit themselves to each other before God. Chinese typically render these commitments to the Heavens and to the Earth. Such relations between the Heavens and the Earth that exist in Chinese culture provide a fascinating insight into the development of Chinese civilization.

Since ancient times, Chinese have all along held the Heavens and the Earth that they live on in great reverence. Thousands of years ago, when many peoples embraced a strong belief in Spirits who were thought of as the creators of all beings, the Chinese had begun to probe into astronomy as well as geography. There an old man for the first time unveiled the laws of nature and formed a cosmic view of worshiping nature, by symbolically comparing the relations between the Heavens and the Earth and men to a chain.

The old man, regarded by the world as

Portrait of Lao Tzu Explaining Tao Te Ching to Yin Xi (partial) by Sheng Maozuo, Yuan Dynasty (1271-1368).

the initiator of the Chinese Taoist school - the native religion of China - was called Lao Tzu.

之必固興之將欲奪之必固興之是謂
弱勝剛強魚不可脫於淵國之利器
不以示人道常無為而無不為侯王若能守
物將自化而欲作吾將鎮之以無名之樸
之樸亦將不欲不欲以靜天下將自正
上德不德是以有德下德不失德是以無
德無為而無以為下德為之而有以為上

Lao Tzu and Taoism

A Journey to the West is the fantastic mythological tale, which rightly occupies a preeminent place amongst the pantheon of classical Chinese literature. Sun Wukong or the Monkey King hero of the tale was a magical being possessed of considerable powers. He was also an incorrigible trickster. When he violated the laws of the Heavens, he was thrown into the so-called Crucible of the Eight Trigrams, where Taishang Laojun, a supernatural God, burned him in alchemical oil for 49 days. Taishang Laojun is none other but Lao Tzu. Ironically, despite such a characterization Lao Tzu himself and his teachings are very much anti-theistic in nature. He laid great emphasis not on supernatural beings in the

Taishang Laojun, a supernatural God, who is in fact Lao Tzu.

Heavens but rather on the laws of nature and dedicated his whole life to seeking after the links in the cosmic chain that bound the Heavens and the Earth.

Taoism is the only spiritual belief system which is native to China. Its ultimate origins are shrouded in the remote mists of history, but Taoism has always been associated with one man who is Lao Tzu.

Taishang Laojun is a respectful name of Lao Tzu in Taoism, the only Chinese native religion. Of the sites cited by the UNESCO as the World Heritages in China, five are associated with Taoism.

In any Taoist area of China, it is common to see a statue of an old man, with white hair and beard, long ears drooping down towards his shoulders. This is the traditional representation of Lao Tzu the man most closely associated with Taoist belief.

Mirages are caused by the reflection

of light. Like wind, rain and lighting they are a natural phenomenon that seem unremarkable to us, living as we do in a world where everything can be explained scientifically. But in ancient times, such phenomena could be understood only in terms of supernatural spirits. They saw the Heavens as a faraway: an incomparably wonderful world, the domain of wandering and various supernatural beings. While fearing and worshipping such supernatural beings people also dreamed themselves of becoming a member of this pantheon one day. But how could this be achieved?

Some said if you prayed reverentially every day facing the Heavens, a supernatural being would come down to the Earth and bring you up to the Heavens; others maintained that by making and eating so-

Lao Tzu

Portrait of Master Zhangtianshi by Fan Yi (Ming Dynasty, 1368-1644).

called immortal pills you could become a supernatural being and fly yourself to the Heavens.

For many thousands of years, the Chinese people subscribed to such beliefs and worshipped a whole galaxy of supernatural

Chinese character reading "Tao".

beings, ghosts and ancestors. Around the middle of the 2nd century BC, a man named Zhang Daoling, came across a book. It was only 5,000 characters long but still Zhang Daoling recognized its all-embracing importance. Zhang, who had been a seventh-rank county magistrate, cherished it as a book of the Heavens, and in his later years, taking this book as the highest holy scripture, founded a sect, to live by the ideas set down in this short book. The book was *Tao Te Ching* and its author was Lao Tzu, and the sect was named "Tao".

We can say that the concept of "Tao" lies at the very heart of Lao Tzu's doctrines, that is to say, all conclusions derive from the idea of "Tao" and all finally are reduced to the idea of "Tao." The original meaning of the Chinese character "Tao" is "a road or path people walk upon," the Tao of Lao Tzu is a sublimation and extension of that meaning.

At the very dawn of Taoism, as an organized spiritual belief system, Taoist master Zhang Daoling gathered together the thoughts about Tao of Lao Tzu, which form the very source of Taoist thought. He also assimilated a wide variety of Chinese traditional folk religious beliefs and the persistent faith of Chinese in supernatural beings into a relatively systematic religion, where Tao was taken as the very essence

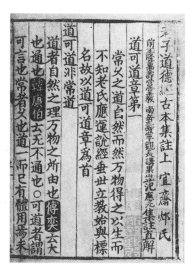

Wood engraved edition of *Tao Te Ching* (Song Dynasty, 960-1279).

of Taoism. And as Lao Tzu was the very living incarnation of Tao, then he naturally became the holiest presiding deity of Chinese Taoism.

之必固興之將欲奪之必固興之是謂微
弱勝剛強魚不可脫於淵國之利器
示人道常無為而無不為侯王若能守
將自化而欲作吾將鎮之以無名之樸
之樸亦將不欲不欲以靜天下將自正
德不德是以有德下德不失德是以無德
無為而無以為下德為之而有以為上

Story of Lao Tzu

As with the founders of all religions and belief systems, it is almost impossible to separate the man from the myth. Accounts of Lao Tzu's birth are a case in point. Some accounts say he was brought to Earth by a shooting star. An even more fabulous story contends that his mother, a countrywoman named Li Shi, was going to wash clothes one day when she found a yellow plum floating down the river. Li Shi fished the fist-sized plum out of the water with a branch and because she felt hot and thirsty, ate it immediately. To her surprise, and no doubt to the surprise of anyone she had to explain it to, the young girl fell pregnant after eating the plum.

This, however, was no ordinary

pregnancy. Li Shi carried the child for a full 81 years until one day in the first month of spring, a full eight decades after consuming the fateful plum, the sky suddenly was lit up with sheet after sheet of lightning and thunder rent the still spring air. With the clouds fantastically darkening overhead, Li Shi collapsed in pain under a plum tree, and soon after the insistent wailing of a new born baby told her that her 81-year-long pregnancy was at an end. Bolts of lightning rained down from the Heavens to herald the new arrival and it is said nine black dragons caused immense quantities of rain to fall upon the Earth in order to bathe and clean the baby. Legend says that these dragons became the nine divine wells that remained on Earth to mark the spot where the divine Lao Tzu entered the world of men. This, of course, was no ordinary new-born baby. Legend has it that when he was

Lao Tzu

Legend has it that when Lao Tzu was born, he was already an old man.

born, he was already an old man with white hair and a beard and so his mother gave him the name, Lao Tzu, which means "Old Son" (as Tzu can also mean son in Chinese).

One does not, of course, have to take such stories as literal truth. Many commentators have pointed out the symbolism of the story: the yellow plum - yellow is closely associated with Taoism; Taoism holds that "one bears two, two bears three, and three bears all things on Earth," and so three is seen as a most powerful number, three to the power of four gives you eighty-one, the number of years Lao Tzu is said to have lived in his mother's belly. As with Christianity and indeed all other religious beliefs there is an ocean of symbolic and metaphorical meaning hidden in seemingly outlandish legends.

When Lao Tzu was born, it was the fifteenth day of the second Chinese lunar month. Every year, on this day, strains of music and drumbeats accompany the chanting of scriptures echo loudly into the skies above Taoist temples everywhere; devoted Taoist disciples dress in formal regalia to celebrate the birthday of their founding father.

A young Chinese Taoist named Zhou

A grand ceremony was held in Quanzhou of Fujian Province to mark the birthday of Lao Tzu.

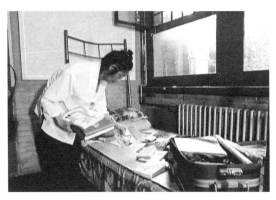

Zhou Shuangliu, a Chinese Taoist.

Shuangliu has visited almost all the Taoist holy lands of China since he left his hometown in Guizhou ten years ago. The first thing he does on arrival at a new place is to collect the local versions of the *Tao Te Ching*. To date he has amassed almost 500 versions. This project stems from the young Taoist's worship of Lao Tzu, a reverence that has led him to choose this special life. His dream is to found a "Tao Te Ching College" in his hometown Guizhou, and to introduce the long standing Taoist culture

Tao Te Ching editions on view.

to Chinese as well as to foreigners from all over the world who are interested in this great cultural legacy.

Today, when pious men and women prostrate themselves at the feet of the Superior Old God, praying for well-being and happiness, some do not realise he was once a man of flesh and blood and that the religious scriptures the Taoist disciples

Visitors to a temple fair of the Beijing White Cloud Temple.

are chanting are from the *Tao Te Ching*, the book that Lao Tzu handed down as his great legacy. The existence of this great book is the firmest evidence that a man called Lao Tzu did indeed once exist.

One bears two, two bears three, and three bears all the things of the world; the Earth imitates the Heavens, the Heavens bears the Tao, and the Tao is Nature....

Indeed, it is true that all founders of the world's great religions were real men, Sakyamuni, Muhammad, and Jesus Christ being three of the most notable examples. They were all effectively deified by their followers after their death. After his death, Lao Tzu became known as the Superior Old God, but as the human founder of the Taoist school, people seldom were aware of his real name and the events of his very much human life.

歙之必固張之將欲弱之必固興之是謂
微明柔弱勝剛強魚不可脫於淵國之利器
不可以示人道常無為而無不為侯王若能守
萬物將自化化而欲作吾將鎮之以無名之樸
無名之樸亦將不欲不欲以靜天下將自正
上德不德是以有德下德不失德是以無
德無為而無以為下德為之而有以為上

Lao Tzu in History Books

What can we know for sure about the life of this man who lived over two millennia over? A mere 400 ambiguous Chinese characters have been set down in the great Chinese historical chronicles written by Sima Qian, Ancient China's most revered master of history, over 2000 years ago. These 400 characters constitute for us the most authoritative and earliest historical clues available to us in our quest to unravel the mysteries of the life and times of the first ancestor of Taoism.

According to the records, the family name of Lao Tzu was not Lao but Li, and his personal name was Er, hence the name Li Er in most modern literature. And in accordance with Chinese naming

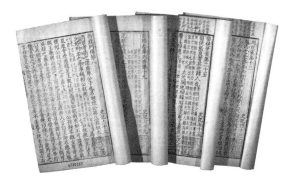

Historical Records.

principles, he also had a further courtesy name, Dan, which in fact means "big ears." As a sage of Ancient Chinese times, many and varying historical and cultural roles have been imposed on Lao Tzu: firstly, he was the Father of Chinese Philosophy; secondly he was the progenitor of Taoism. His existence for us seems to maddeningly fluctuate between that of a god and of a man. As the chronicles record, he was "like a supernatural dragon with only the head and never the tail can be discerned."

Lao Tzu

Taiji Palace in Luyi of Henan Province was where Lao Tzu was born.

Can we say with any certainty where Lao Tzu, or Li Er, was born 2,500 years ago? Controversy continues to rage about where in fact can be said to be the home of the great sage. The two most likely contenders would seem to be Qurenli in Kuxian County of the then Chu State (modern-day Luyi County in Henan Province) and Woyang County, which is less than 100 km away, in modern-day Anhui Province.

Lao Tzu in History Books

Lao Tzu.

In Luyi County, during the Han Dynasty (206 BC-220 AD) a temple honouring Lao Tzu, was constructed, which was centuries later during the Tang Dynasty (618-907) referred to as the Taiqing Palace. The Tang rulers claimed Lao Tzu as a direct descendant of the ruling Tang dynasty. This location has become commonly associated in the popular imagination with the birthplace of the founder of Taoism.

Archaeological surveys jointly sponsored by the State Administration of Cultural Relics and relevant departments of cultural relics of Henan Province on the palace have been carried out. Although the only visible relics of the site now date from the Qing Dynasty (1616-1911), below ground are to be found the archaeological remains from many different eras and dynasties, including the Tang and the Song. The archaeological survey revealed a site which had been the scene of sacred offerings by different dynasties stretching back almost 2,000 years which would seem to support the contention that it was indeed a place of great importance and perhaps indeed the birthplace of the great sage.

Over the course of some 1,900 years, three emperors successively come here to offer personal sacrifice to Lao Tzu. The foundation of the Tang Dynasty (618-907) ushered in the era most closely associated with Lao Tzu and Taoism: the emperor's father was converted to Taoism one night. Because Lao Tzu and the emperors of the Tang Dynasty shared, the same family

Laojuntai in Luyi County of Henan Province is also called Shengxiantai, meaning place where Lao Tzu demised and rose to the Heavens. As a matter of fact, this was where Lao Tzu gave lectures in his late years.

name, Lao Tzu himself was incorporated as a direct ancestor of the ruling Li family. The Taiqing Palace of Luyi County was officially recognized as the royal family temple and gained great prestige. It was enlarged on a large scale: each side occupied a length of nearly 5 km and there were as many as 600 rooms spread over 20 square km.

In the second year of the reign of Tianbo (743), Li Longji (also known as Tang Emperor Xuanzong), accompanied by his most beloved wife Yang Guifei, even came to Luyi to pay his respects to his ancestor. And to commemorate the long pilgrimage, he had a ceremonial stele erected - *The Stele to Commemorate Tang Xuanzong's Commentary on the Tao Te Ching.*

From that year on, on the 15th day of the second month in the Chinese lunar calendar every year, Taoists, pilgrims, merchants as well as common people from

A grand ceremony was held in the hometown of Lao Tzu, Luyi County of Henan Province, to mark the birthday of Lao Tzu.

hundreds of kilometres away would gather at the Taiqing Palace Fair of Luyi County performing various memorial activities to pay their respects to Lao Tzu. Such customs have lasted over a thousand years. The local people are immensely proud of their eminent ancestor. They think peace and happiness will come their way given his influence in the Heavens. Invariably locals set a sculpture of Lao Tzu in the center of their main room or hang a picture of him on the wall.

Pei Xianwen, a resident of Luyi, is famous for the sculptures of Lao Tzu that he produces. Every tourist season, many people commission Lao Tzu sculptures from him. Since the Taiqing Palace has come to be acknowledged as the physical and spiritual homeland of Lao Tzu, it is naturally believed that a statue of the master in his home place has much greater value than one produced elsewhere. Indeed for many Taoists, a statue from any other place simply will not do. Pei Xianwen is certainly not complaining.

Then, what did Lao Tzu himself look like 2500 years ago on the Earth? People of today can only imagine and conjecture his appearance by the description of artists. But how the image of Lao Tzu in paintings

Pei Xianwen in Luyi County of Henan Province, who is distinguished in making sculptures of Lao Tzu.

was handed down?

In Chinese eyes, Lao Tzu is first and foremost an ancient philosopher with unrivalled insight and wisdom; in the eyes of the adherents of Taoism, Lao Tzu is an individual intrinsically associated with the Nature; as someone who succeeded in eliminating desire; and in the eyes of many common people, he is a man with white eyebrows, white hair and white beard. The

Stone sculptures at the Qingyuan Mountain, Quanzhou, Fujian Province.

most remarkable bodily feature noted by people is a man with "nose which is like a pillar, ears which reach the shoulders and arms which can extend to the knees."

This is another illustration of the half man, half-god status of Lao Tzu. He was most definitely distinct from common people in appearance. The ears down to the shoulder just means his ears were extraordinarily big, which, according to Chinese traditional physiognomy, was a symbol of good luck. Lao Tzu may indeed have been a fortunate man in his real life; however, in another sense as a supernatural entity and progenitor of a great spiritual system he is without rival.

The 6th century BC was a time of enormous political, social, spiritual and philosophical ferment. It was a time when China was in the midst of a long and difficult transition of social organization.

It was a time of almost constant warfare as a patchwork assortment of states sought glory and hegemony on the battlefield. This was also a time of enormous intellectual innovation and disputation. Hundreds of schools contended the great spiritual questions of the age, a time of speculation and questioning. The ancient chronicles contend that Lao Tzu's father was Li Qian, a petty functionary who provided his son with a good education.

Some years later Lao Tzu came with his father to Luoyang in Henan, which was then the capital of the State of Zhou Dynasty(1046 BC-770 BC). Walking through the streets of modern-day Luoyang, and standing on the steps of the city's temple, one can perhaps catch the merest taste of what the city must have been all those thousands of years ago: the heated disputation on academic subjects, about the Heavens and Earth and man's place in the scheme of things. It was in Luoyang that Lao Tzu found employment as the keeper of the royal archives, a position that allowed the voraciously curious young man to absorb all sorts of knowledge and learning from the vast array of tomes that made up the king's

Qiyun Pagoda in Baima Temple in Luoyang, Henan Province.

library and archive.

One of Lao Tzu's duties was said to be keeping a record of the various meetings which daily took place between the king and the various ministers and attendants who made up the royal court. At such meetings, a strict protocol was observed, and the only one who was permitted to sit was the king himself. However a special privilege was granted to the learned scribe. While transcribing the minutes of all royal appointments, Lao Tzu was permitted to lean against a large pillar in the royal chamber. This is the origin of the position "Functionary under the Pillar" which was extensively used by later generations to denote such a post.

Today, almost all Taoist temples include just such an iron pillar in their structures to commemorate Lao Tzu's work as a "Functionary under the Pillar." There is,

Lao Tzu once worked as a government secretary.

predictably, a much more fabulous story of the origin of this pillar, which is widely referred to by many common people as the "Driving Mountain Whip."

Luyi County was, in antiquity, known by the name of "Kudi" (meaning "Bitter Land)." This was because the land at that time was said to be barren, mountainous and covered in impenetrable forest with wild beasts wandering the slopes, making it an extremely hazardous place for human habitation. Legend says that Lao Tzu was determined to improve the land of his birth and so he smelted ores for seven days and nights to produce extremely durable wrought iron, which he then spent another 49 days fashioning into a mystic whip of unimaginable power. The divine sage raised the whip and smote the mountain three times, each time throwing up dazzling flashes of lightning and blinding fire.

The mountains disintegrated and in their stead was left a fertile, flat land where people could live and work in comfort and contentment. The pillar in most Taoist temples is thus believed to be a commemoration of these godlike feats by Lao Tzu.

Today, Lao Tzu is greatly honored by Chinese blacksmiths and those who work metal and iron. He can be seen as the "patron saint" of this profession in much the same way as Chinese carpenters regard the famous Lu Ban. Today in Luyi County, a custom persists among the local people of performing what is known as the "Forging Iron Dance," which is a celebration and a commemoration of the Great Sage's skill in metalworking.

As the popular ballad goes: "Firstly beat the iron, secondly beat the steel, thirdly strike a sickle, fourthly strike a spear,

Portrait of Taishang Laojun.

fifthly light a fire, sixthly sift the charcoal, seventhly forge a hoe, eighthly forge a sword, ninthly forge a crescent axe, and tenthly forge an adamant drill, adamant drill...."

Depressing as it may be, it seems a feature common to many cultures that great advances in metalworking are invariably first manifested in the production of more sophisticated and destructive weapons. Such developments made the turbulent days of the Spring and Autumn Period (770 BC-476 BC) in ancient China even more unstable. Internecine warfare broke out among the Zhou Dynasty (11th century BC-256 BC) hierarchy. In 516 BC, it is recorded that a vanquished Zhou prince, his political and military ambitions stymied in his homeland, fled to the State of Chu, carrying with him the greatest and most valuable books and archives that made up the royal library. It is said that Lao Tzu couldn't bear the loss of so many of the precious volumes which he had cared for so lovingly. It is said he retired from official duties and returned to a simple life in his homeland.

A local opera item known as the Henan Zhuizi tells the story of the meeting between the two great masters of Chinese civilization, Confucius and Lao Tzu. It is said Confucius asking Lao Tzu about the performance of rites recorded in the *Historical Records* is held by most modern scholars to be credible. Lao Tzu and Confucius lived in the same period, but Lao Tzu was 20 years older than Confucius. According to historical records, they met three times, twice in Lao Tzu's hometown. Confucius, whose doctrine and belief were rites and benevolence, had an exchange of views with Lao Tzu who advocated returning to the Nature. The dialogues between the founders of Taoism and Confucianism set in train a process whereby the thoughts of the two

Lao Tzu in History Books

According to historical record, Confucius paid a special visit to Lao Tzu, then aged 62, in present-day Luoyang of Henan Province. This meeting proved to be important for Confucius to build up his ideological system.

schools commingled and could develop harmoniously in later ages.

Though each of the two had their own individual beliefs in terms of how best the world might be morally improved, Confucius still greatly appreciated Lao Tzu's erudition and deep thoughts. He even compared Lao Tzu to a dragon, incomprehensible and ineffable. Gazing on a flowing spring river, Confucius observed: "The passage of time is just like the flow of water, which goes on day and night," while Lao Tzu observed: "The supreme god is like water, which nourishes all things without trying to."

The river that crosses Luyi County from west to east has been flowing silently across the land for thousands of years. It is the Wohe River. At the beginning of the 6th century, the ancient geographer Li Daoyuan, after visiting Lao Tzu's hometown, described it thus: The Wohe River lies to the south of Luyi. However, judging from the geographic position of today's Taiqing Palace, the Wohe River is exactly to the north, which thus has recently raised further questions over the birthplace of Lao Tzu.

Lao Tzu has for millennia slept the sleep of ages and would be quite amazed and no doubt quite amused by the fact that people over 2,500 years after his death should be

Scene of Wohe River.

Baiyunguan in Beijing is the chief temple of the Quanzhen Taoist Sect and center for the Longmen Subsect. It is now the site of the China Taoist Association. According to historical records, Tang Emperor Xuanzong (685-762) built a stone statue of the seated figure of Lao Tzu and a temple known as the Tianchang Temple to enshrine it. After the Jin Dynasty (1115-1234), it was renamed Taiji Palace and Changchun Palace. In the early days of the Ming Dynasty (1368-1644), it was named Baiyunguan Temple. The existing Baiyunguan Hall was built during the Ming Dynasty.

still heatedly and ceaselessly arguing about the exact location of his birthplace, which to the Great Sage would see as utterly meaningless. What really matters is, he has passed on his thoughts to the people and the Taoism he created and constructed constitutes a profound philosophical system that has had an enormous influence on the politics, culture, and economic life of China.

微之必固興之將欲奪之必固與之是謂
示弱勝剛強魚不可脫於淵國之利器
不以示人道常無為而無不為侯王若能守
之萬物將自化化而欲作吾將鎮之以無名之樸
無名之樸亦將不欲不欲以靜天下將自正
上德不德是以有德下德不失德是以無德
上德無為而無以為下德為之而有以為上

Lao Tzu and Chinese Culture

China's most eminent writer of modern times, Lu Xun, once observed: "One who hasn't read the *Tao Te Ching* cannot have any real understanding of Chinese culture." An impressive claim which surely begs the question: how exactly did it influence Chinese civilization and culture? For thousands of years, perhaps all ancient civilizations ultimately became submerged in the long river of history. This never happened with Chinese civilization. The civilization and culture, like an aged but still flourishing oak tree, is still vigorous after the ravages of wind and rain. But where does this vigorous life force come from?

Water is the most common constituent

element of the planet human beings live on; indeed it is the ultimate source of all life on that planet. Lao Tzu held the character of water to be most virtuous. It nourishes all beings but never contends with them. Water has always been an important element flowing in the veins of Chinese culture these last 5,000 years.

The influence of Taoism pervades every single aspect of Chinese culture. Take Chinese painting for example. Traditional Chinese painting takes white and black as its principal tones. These colours contain within the extremes they represent all other colours: they are the bookends to riotous profusion of colour that nature offers.

The element of water is as central to Chinese painting as it is to Taoist ideas. Indeed water functioned as an explanatory method for many ancient philosophers as they sought to expound their views on the world. Fluid and dynamic, water assimilates all colours to itself, while itself being colourless; transparent. The colour without colour is the greatest colour, a paradox that fits in well with Lao Tzu's gnomic observations: "A greatest shape has no shape; the loudest voice sounds soft." Hence the choice of water as a colorless solvent in Chinese traditional paintings. It neutralizes all colors and dyestuffs.

The ambiguous linkages between questions of morality and propriety and the elegant, opaque, suggestiveness of expression bestow a unique charm on Chinese paintings: which are representations of reality yet they transcend reality. Dark ink and heavy color evoke weight and strength while the outline evokes a sense of ease and gentleness. Such subtle delight also ultimately derives

Ink and wash painting by modern Chinese artist Huang Binhong (1865-1955).

from water. Chinese painting cherishes water as its blood and ink as its gold just as traditional Taoism regards life as supported by *qi* and blood. To Chinese paintings the rhythm of *qi* is also vital. Drawing inspiration from *qi* and water and treating paintings as living entities, Chinese painters achieve a unique combination of evocative beauty. This is the clearest manifestation of the Taoist maxim: "The supreme good is like water, which nourishes all things without trying to."

According to Lao Tzu, water is the softest element but simultaneously also the most powerful. One need only gaze at the magnificent and majestic mountains and valleys, which are carved out over millennia by water's relentless force. That a constant drip can wear through a stone is a fundamentally important Taoist concept. What appears weak eventually conquers what appears strong. This idea is vividly demonstrated in the ancient Chinese art of *tai chi*. Softness lies at the very essence of Chinese *tai chi*. Relaxation of limbs combines with slow and gentle movements creating an extreme softness which develops into a powerful force: thus the weak can conquer the strong. *Tai chi* tempers force with grace, yin with yang and rapidity with slowness as well as controlling movement with softness. One could describe it like cotton wool wrapped around a core of steel. The practice is founded on the performance of a succession of movements: one move connects to

Autumn River Water by Ma Yuan (Song Dynasty, 960-1279).

Chinese *tai chi* shadow boxing.

another; the force may pause but the will is ever present. The fluid movements of the body flow gracefully like the spinning of the silkworm, like drifting clouds and flowing water. In the realm of a *tai chi* master, there are no others in the world but himself. The interior and exterior worlds combine, so an accomplished *tai chi* master coexist between the Earth and the Heavens.

Chinese traditional music too has been significantly influenced by the Taoism popularized by Lao Tzu. This music comes from Jiangnan (areas south of the Yangtze River), which abounds in bamboo and silk: two natural elements which have nourished a branch of Chinese folk music *Jiangnan Sizhu*. Nature is thought of as the source as well as the soul of Chinese folk music. A longing for nature can be discerned in the clear, elegant, natural and harmonious rhythms of Chinese folk songs. This life attitude of respecting and returning to nature has a close parallel with the ideas of Lao Tzu about nature. Thousands of masterpieces of ancient classic music such as *Lofty Mountain and Gushing Cascade, Guangling San, A Moon Is Mirrored in the Second Fountain, Wild Geese Descending on the*

Portrait of Boya Playing Music by Wang Zhenpeng (Yuan Dynasty, 1206-1368).

Sandy Beach, Moonlight over the River in Spring and *The Moon Is High* thematically speaking all have in common an absolute adherence to Lao Tzu's belief that "the Tao is just nature."

In the West, the traditional classical form of music tends to be more magnificent and grandiose than Chinese folk music, which places more emphasis on grace and silence. Lao Tzu always emphasized the importance of "nothingness": a house is suitable to

Taoist music performance.

live in, he observed, just because there is a space in it, that is to say, it is just the "nothingness" that makes a house livable. The flexible and unpredictable nature of Chinese music also comes from this "nothingness." Sudden pauses abound in Chinese music, especially ancient music, which leaves an even larger space to the musicians because the pauses contain much more than mere silence. Such music tends to be artistic, flexible, unpredictable, and imaginative rather than expressionistic.

The Heavens is circular and the Earth is square. This is a traditional characterization of nature in ancient Chinese philosophy. The game of go is a graphic illustration of such ideas. The board is square, symbolizing the Earth, while the pieces are round, symbolizing the Heavens. There are 361 junctions on the board which approximates to 365 days in a year.

The Chinese people worshipped nature in ancient times and thus they created such a form of entertainment as an illustration and a symbol of their views on the Heavens and the Earth and nature. The board is simply drawn with horizontal and perpendicular lines while the pieces are divided into white and black. It was not only an entertaining game but also functioned as an important symbol of yin and yang, the two opposing forces of nature. That the game of go

Go games unearthed from Zouxian County, Shandong Province (Ming Dynasty, 1368-1644).

has become a worldwide phenomenon is because it is different from any other games like chess or checkers. There are no pieces more powerful than any others; all pieces are simply either white or black, but from them endless variations result. Of all games, the properties and rules of the game of go are the simplest, but endless variation inevitably results. This again echoes a central tenet of Taoist teaching: "The Tao bears one; one bears two; two bears three; three bears all the things of the world." The game of go also starts from the simplest

Playing Chess found in the Tomb of Zhang in Turpan, Xinjiang (early Tang Dynasty, 618-907).

movements and then produces boundless complex variations.

These traditional arts that have taken deep root in the Chinese culture are endowed with identifiably Chinese characteristics. These characteristics are undoubtedly a reflection of the natural philosophies that lie at the core of the Taoist thought of Lao Tzu. Of all ages, Taoist ideas have invested Chinese culture and art with a unique, exquisite tone as well as an aesthetic beauty that places emphasis on inner spirit rather than on outward forms.

As the master Lao Tzu said: "The Tao that can be named is not the eternal Tao; the names that can be named are not the eternal names…."

之必固興之將欲奪之必固與之是謂微明弱勝剛強魚不可脫於淵國之利器不可以示人道常無為而無不為侯王若能守之萬物將自化化而欲作吾將鎮之以無名之樸無名之樸亦將不欲不欲以靜天下將自正上德不德是以有德下德不失德是以無德上德無為而無以為下德為之而有以為上仁

Lao Tzu's Theory of Government

In the minds of common people, Lao Tzu was just a free and easy scholar riding on the back of a black ox. During his life he was never appointed to high office: nor did he have the ear of any eminent king. However, he succeeded in adumbrating a blueprint for the carrying out of state affairs, which would have an enormous influence on a large number of Chinese dynasties. This system was known as "Wu Wei," and was essentially a laissezfaire philosophy of non-enforcement for the management of state affairs.

The wisdom of Taoism has been often compared to the moon by many scholars. The sun is majestic and powerful; we cannot look straight at the sun because of its brilliance and we are somewhat awestruck in the face of its awesome power. By contrast, the moon is altogether more gentle and mild. It inspires in us feelings of quietude and peacefulness.

Wood carving of *Lecturing Lao Tzu* by Wu Xiaoyang.

Horizontal board inscribed with "Wu Wei" written by Qing (1616-1911) Emperor Kangxi (1654-1722) in the Palace Museum in Beijing.

Lao Tzu advocated self-cultivation and self-rectification, which means that the rulers of a country should have faith in the people. Human nature he saw as essentially honest and true. If this nature was allowed to unfold, the state would be naturally a well administered state. This is the essence of Lao Tzu's "Wu Wei" theory of government: "Non-enforcement and non-contention."

One interesting characteristic of Chinese history was the invariable pattern that emerged where a time of peace would be followed by one of riotous disorder and vice versa. A long period of union inevitably led to a split while a long period of atomized disunity inexorably culminated in reunion. In history Taoism often played an important role in the regular process of pacification and reunification.

Some 2,200 years ago, after many years of wars and strife, Liu Bang, a leader of the rebel peasant force eventually won a decisive victory and the bitterness of the war was ended with the beginning of the reign of the Han Dynasty (206 BC-220 AD). It was indeed a serious challenge for a leader to bring his people out of such troubled times and bring about revitalization. Some years later, a man called Cao Can was called into the royal palace to replace the former prime minister Xiao He. Before long, people found very little had changed: the old rules were still observed even though the prime minister's residence had a new master. Cao Can had much more affection for inns and taverns than for legislative assemblies and palaces. The emperor was puzzled. Cao Can explained that the laws and regulations had been adequate since the time of Liu Bang and Xiao He had succeeded in pacifying the state. All they needed to do was just to follow the rules rather than attempting any complex and potentially disastrous reform of the rules. Cao Can was the first prime minister to administered state affairs in line with the ideas of "Wu Wei" in Chinese

Portrait of Lao Tzu Riding on the Back of a Black Ox by Zhang Lu of the Ming Dynasty (1368-1644), collected by the Imperial Palace Museum in Taipei, Taiwan.

history. This was indeed a refreshing development in the political field and it brought great stability and prosperity to the country.

The first monarch who deliberately adopted the policy of "Ruling by Wu Wei" was Liu Heng, the fourth son of Liu Bang and the third emperor who came to power in 180 BC. Before acceding to the throne, a major outbreak of civil strife had just been quelled. The first thing Liu Heng did after his succession was to abolish the widespread practice of torture and to thoroughly reform the rural taxation system. This was a time when, it was said, every 8,000 common people supported only one official and thus the burden on the grassroots was greatly relieved by Liu Heng's farsighted reforms.

The reign of Liu Heng was immortalized as the very "pinnacle of Wen and Jing." During his reign, taxes upon peasants

Lao Tzu's Theory of Government

"Govern by doing nothing that goes against nature" is a policy that allows the people to live in peace and happiness.

were only 3 percent and would be often exempted when bad harvests occurred. Liu Heng's policies created a strong country and a prosperous nation. After that period of national prosperity, there was said to be so much money in the warehouse that some gold hadn't even been taken out and used before the strings that secured the bags had rotted away.

In the 7th and the 8th centuries, China during the Tang Dynasty (618-907) entered into an age of peace and prosperity and for the first time led the world. The merits attributed to the second emperor Li Shimin who ascended the throne in 626 were many and various. He adopted a set of "Quietude" and "Wu Wei" policies popular with the common people. A famous Silver Age in history was created. Li once said: "Managing the country is like planting a tree. Branches and leaves will grow freely only when the root is secure. When the emperor is free, the common people will also live and work in peace and contentment."

The most notable adherent of Taoism during the Tang Dynasty was the emperor, Li Longji (also known as Tang Xuanzong) who came to power in 712. Before his succession, the Tang Empire had come close to collapse and ruin, because of the policies pursued by Li's grandmother Wu Zetian who had greedily grasped power. After Li Longji mounted the throne, he deliberately promoted Taoism in the administering of state affairs and enabled the dynasty to recover rapidly after decades of civil strife. Li Longji, the fifth emperor of the Tang Dynasty, was also the first emperor in Chinese history to personally annotate the *Tao Te Ching*. The country entered an unprecedented era of power and splendor during his reign. Taoism contributed towards a new era of development after Li Longji. Modern scholar Yan Lingfeng has calculated that since the Eastern Han Dynasty (25-220), there have been over 1,600 kinds of writings about Lao Tzu, while in recent years, various annotated versions of the *Tao Te Ching* still emerge every year: ample testimony to the persistent relevance of this work.

The famous *Carved Translation of the Tao Te Ching was* carved by Pan Youquan, an 80 year old man. Pan used to teach world history in a middle school. He has a wide range of hobbies. Of them, painting, calligraphy and seal cutting are his especial passions, an essential part of his life for five to six decades. After retirement, his overriding passion is to promote Lao Tzu to the world.

When Pan was 60, he tried to carve two small seals on the day of Lao Tzu's birthday.

Lao Tzu's Theory of Government

Carved Translation of the Tao Te Ching.

A flash of inspiration struck: considering that he was a countryman of Lao Tzu and loved carving so much why not carve the entire original text of the *Tao Te Ching*. People could appreciate his craftsmanship and simultaneously, learn more about the great Sage and his teachings.

Seals inscribed with *Tao Te Ching* of Pan Youquan.

When Pan started the carving he was in his 60s. It was a monumental undertaking to carve all 5,000 characters of the *Tao Te Ching* on stones of varying shapes and sizes.

After he had finished carving, the result was not very satisfactory to Pan, so he just smoothed the stone and started carving again. Eventually, Pan realized his great dream, namely turning the *Tao Te Ching* into over 700 stone seals of various sizes, on the eve of Lao Tzu's birthday anniversary in 1993 after six years' of remarkable effort. Eight times Pan was not happy with the

final product. Eight times he began again. The carving in the end used up some 2,000 stones.

未弱勝剛強魚不可脫於淵國之利器不以示人道常無為而無不為侯王若能守物將自化化而欲作吾將鎮之以無名之樸名之樸亦將不欲不欲以靜天下將自正上德不德是以有德下德不失德是以無德上德無為而無以為下德為之而有以為上

Influence on the World

In 1988, the then president of America Ronald Reagan quoted Lao Tzu in his *State of the Union*, saying "governing a great nation is like cooking a small fish; do not overdo it." How could it be that a Christian president of the United States should come to quote an old man who lived in China 2,500 years ago. Perhaps this interest in the teachings of Lao Tzu is due to its pacifist philosophy. In a troubled century, as the 20th century most definitely was, people naturally turn to a voice of

US President Ronald Reagon (1911-2004).

peace and ideas of calm amid the clamour of war.

Most Westerners learn about Lao Tzu from the *Tao Te Ching*. The first edition in Europe was the French version translated by Stanislas Julien and published in Paris in 1842. Soon after that, German and English versions began to appear. Julien's French translation caused enormous diagreement. Another Frenchman claimed to have already translated the work indeed claiming that Julien had plagiarized his work. It was a fierce dispute and lasted all of 15 years.

One of Russia's most famous writers, Tolstoy knew of Lao Tzu through the French version of the *Tao Te Ching*. It

French edition of *Tao Te Ching*.

Taoist representatives from various corners of the world gathered at the cultural relics hall of the Kowloon Park in Hong Kong, where various editions of the *Tao Te Ching* are on view.

was to have a profound influence on his philosophy of life. On March 10, 1884, Tolstoy wrote in his diary: "People should conduct themselves like water as Lao Tzu said. The water runs forward when there

Foreign tourists visiting Baiyunguan Temple in Beijing.

is no obstacle ahead. When it meets a dike, it stops. When a gap occurs in the dike, the water continues on its course. It becomes square in a square container and becomes round in a round container. Thus the water is more important than all things and stronger than all things."

Foreign Taoists in the Baiyunguan Temple.

After World War I, William II, the then emperor of the defeated Germany, sighed with great emotion after reading the *Tao Te Ching* for the first time. "If only I have read the book earlier! Perhaps world history could have been rewritten." United Nations statistics show that among all the cultural classics in the world, the *Tao Te Ching* is second only to the *Bible* in terms of circulation of translated copies. The *Tao Te*

Influence on the World

English edition of *Holy Bible*.

English edition of the *Tao Te Ching*.

Ching has broken the boundaries of nations and countries and attracted global attention and recognition. The *New York Times* recently voted Lao Tzu first of the ten greatest ancient writers of the world.

微之必固興之將欲奪之必固興之是謂弱勝剛強魚不可脫於淵國之利器不以示人道常無為而無不為侯王若能守之萬物將自化化而欲作吾將鎮之以無名之樸之樸亦將不欲不欲以靜天下將自正上德不德是以有德下德不失德是以無德上德無為而無以為下德為之而有以為上

Tao Te Ching

The story of how the *Tao Te Ching* came to be composed is a well-known story. In 492 BC, round about the demise of the Eastern Zhou Dynasty (770 BC-256 BC) and the catastrophic series of wars that that involved, Lao Tzu, by then a very aged man, resolved to depart from worldly contentions. Legend has it that he sat astride a black ox, with purple mist all around him as he wound his way through the mountains of west Henan. The well-known Chinese idiom "From the east comes the purple mist" derives from this journey and the motto adorns the doorways of countless Chinese families even today. Hangu Pass is a high mountain passage, which connects the Central Plains with the

Yin Xi asked Lao Tzu to explain the key to the *Tao Te Ching*.

western Qinling Mountains. Facing a vast plateau to the west, a steep gully to the east, the Qinling Mountains to the south, and the Yellow River to the north, the remote fortress of Hangu Pass, famous even 2,500 years ago, is where most Chinese people believe that Lao Tzu committed to writing the 5,000 or so characters that constitute the eternal wisdom of the *Tao Te Ching*. The story of how this came to pass is legendary.

The chief guard posted at the border crossing was a man of unusually high education. He was named Yin Xi, and was said to be somewhat of a scholar, astronomy being among his many areas of interest and no little expertise. One day, while scanning the eastern horizons, he espied a faint bloom of purple mist rising from the eastern hills. He took it as a propitious omen and informed his subordinates that it meant that a man of great spiritual learning would soon pass. Thus when Lao Tzu arrived at the Hangu Pass several days later on his black ox he was expected.

The elderly sage sought passage to the western lands but Yin Xi would not let him pass. He knew that this aged holy man was a living repository of spiritual wisdom and teaching and to allow such a treasure to depart from the world of men without passing on something of his learning would be a most terrible crime. He implored the old man to pause a while and set down the essential ideas of his wisdom. Lao Tzu, at first resistant to the guard's pleas eventually relented and thus one of the greatest treasures of Chinese and indeed human civilization came to be produced, the *Tao Te Ching*.

Facing the eternal flow of the great Yellow River, Lao Tzu gathered his thoughts, and sought a means to define that which was undefinable, describe something that defied description and outline something that was intangible and infinite. This he termed the "Tao": A force that existed before the universe; a force that brought the universe into existence; a force that sustained and sustains that universe. The Tao: The way. Gazing at the brilliant moon perched in the Heavens, the old man pondered over the relationship between this force and human beings. That which cannot be rendered using mere words was fashioned into a philosophical poem numbering only 5,000 or so characters. Although Lao Tzu would no doubt have chuckled at the grand notion, the essential ideas of Taoism had been preserved for future generations, and a major foundation stone of Chinese civilization had been set in place. His duty done, Yin Xi let the old man pass and as he slowly rounded the corner on his black ox,

Lao Tzu Working *on Tao Te Ching*.

he was never again seen by human eyes.

Today, as people read through the wisdom contained in the *Tao Te Ching*, they may not pay much attention to its author. Nevertheless the influence of this man is beyond calculation. The rays reflected by his thoughts have already shined upon the inner world of the modern people of the entire planet. And in today's China, the old adages still radiating with the same undimmed light of philosophy and wisdom that burned so brightly two millennia ago. "The net of the Heavens has large meshes, but it lets nothing through," "A journey of a thousand miles begins with a single step," and "Great minds mature slowly" are not only absolutely familiar to Chinese people but indeed to all the people of the world and will in the future, be handed down from one generation to the next.

Our great legacy from the wise old man

is the *Tao Te Ching*, but Lao Tzu has gone. Along the arduous mountain path, he trod a journey to the west. Where has he gone? How many years has he lived? Even the historian Sima Qian did not know his ending. However, people know, we know, his thoughts are still with us; his soul has rooted itself deeply in the boundless space between the Heavens and the Earth; and his wisdom endures in the minds and hearts of millions of people living on the Earth today. The story of his riding a black ox and passing the Hangu Pass will never be forgotten: son shall hear from father and shall in turn pass it on to his son. It was always thus and always thus shall be.

Lao Tzu Riding on the Back of a Black Ox by Yi Ming (Ming Dynasty, 1368-1644).

傲之必固興之將欲奪之必固與之是謂
柔弱勝剛強魚不可脫於淵國之利器
可以示人道常無為而無不為侯王若能守
物將自化化而欲作吾將鎮之以無名之樸
之樸亦將不欲不欲以靜天下將自正
上德不德是以有德下德不失德是以無
德無為而無以為下德為之而有以為上仁

Famous Sayings from 'Tao Te Ching'

The Sage Works to Do Nothing

The divine law may be spoken of, but it is not the common law. Things may be named, but names are not the things.

The highest good is like water. Water benefits everything by giving without taking or contending. It likes the place others dislike, so it follows closely the divine law.

Don't hold your fill but refrain from excess. A whetted and sharpened sword cannot be sharp for ever. A houseful of gold and jade cannot be safeguarded.

Arrogance of wealth and power will bring ruin. Withdrawal after success conforms to the divine law.

Ruling over the present with the law of the past, you can know the beginning of antiquity. Such is the rule of the divine law.

Man imitates earth, earth imitates heaven, heaven follows the divine law, and the divine law follows nature.

The divine law will prevail in the world just as streams flow from the vale to the river and the sea.

As it (the divine law) never claims to be

great, so it becomes great.

The divine law will not interfere, so there is nothing it cannot do.

The divine law may go opposite ways; even weakness is useful. All things in the world come into being with a form; the form comes from the formless.

Having heard the divine law, a good scholar follows it; a common scholar half believes in it; a poor scholar laughs at it. If not laughed at, it cannot be the divine law.

So purity seems soiled, a large square

seems cornerless, a great vessel is the last completed, a great sound is inaudible, a great image is formless, an invisible law is nameless.

One is the child of the divine law. After one come two, after two come three, after three come all things.

The more you know of the human world, the less you know of the divine law. Less and less you need to know till nothing need to be done. When you need do nothing, there is nothing you cannot do. If you need do nothing, then you can rule over the world. If everything need you to do, then you cannot rule over the world.

The great way is even, but people may like the by-path.

The divine law is the key to everything: the treasure for men of virtue, the protection for men without virtue.

In accordance with heaven's divine law, one may win without contending, respond without speaking, come without being summoned. and silent, one may plan well. The Heavens spread a boundless net, and none could escape through its meshes.

The divine law is impartial, but it always favors good men.

Dialectical World

If all men in the world know what is fair, then it is unfair. If all men know what is good, then it is not good.

Thirty spokes radiate from a hub. When there is nothing in the hub, the wheel can roll. Turn clay to make a vessel. When empty, the vessel can be used. Build a room with doors and windows. When empty, the room can be used as dwelling. When there is something, it is beneficial; When empty, it is useful.

☆

The five colors may confuse the eye. The five sounds may deafen the ear. The five tastes may spoil the palate. Riding and hunting may madden the mind. Rare goods may tempt one to do evil.

Stooping, you will be preserved. Wronged, you will be righted. Hollow, you will be filled. Worn out, you will be renewed. Having little, you may gain; having much, you may be at a loss.

Inhale before you exhale! Strengthen what is to be weakened! Raise what is to fall! Give before you take!

The softest thing in the world can penetrate the hardest. There is no space but the matterless can enter. Thus I see the utility of doing nothing.

The teaching by saying nothing and the utility of doing nothing are seldom known to the world.

Perfection does not seem flawless, but it can be used for long. What is full still has vacancy, but it can be used endlessly. The straight may seem crooked; the most skillful may seem clumsy; the most eloquent may seem slow of speech. Be calm rather than rash; be cool rather than hot. Serenity is the right way in the world.

Anything past its prime will decline. If you think it not in the right way, you would be wrong.

☆

Those who know do not speak; those who speak do not know.

☆

Weal comes after woe; woe lies under weal. Who knows the line of demarcation? There is no absolute norm.

☆

The sea can lord it over all the streams flowing from the vales, for it takes a lower position, so water flows into it from hundreds of vales.

☆

A good warrior is not violent, a good fighter is not angry, a good victor will not yield, a good leader will be humble.

Man is born soft and weak; dead, he becomes hard and stiff. Grass and wood grow soft and supple; dead, they become dry and withered. So the hard and strong belong to death; the soft and weak belong to life. Therefore a strong army will be annihilated; a sturdy tree will be cut down. The soft and weak have the upper hand of the hard and strong.

Nothing in the world is softer and weaker than water, but nothing is better to win over the hard and the strong, for it cannot be replaced. The weak may surpass the strong. and the soft may surpass the hard. It is well-known to the world, but none can put it into practice. That is the reason why the sage says:

"Who can bear the humiliation of a state may become its master; who can endure the disaster of a state may become its ruler." It seems wrong, but it is right.

Truthful words may not be beautiful; beautiful words may not be truthful. A good man need not justify himself; who justifies himself may not be a good man. A wise man may not be learned; a learned man may not be wise. A sage does not keep things for himself. The more he helps others, the more he still has. The more he gives, the more he keeps. The divine law will do all good and no harm. The way of a sage is to do what he can but contend with none.

On Ruling a Country

Therefore, the sage does everything without interference, teaches everyone without persuasion, and lets everything begin uninitiated and grow unpossessed. Everything is done without being his deed, and succeeds without being his success.

Honor on man so that none would contend for honor. Value no rare goods so that none would steal or rob. Display nothing desirable lest people be tempted and disturbed.

The Heavens and the Earth are ruthless, they treat everything as straw or dog. The sage is ruthless, he treats everyone as straw or dog.

Those who follow the divine law to serve the ruler will not conquer the world by force. Conquerors will be conquered in turn. Where goes the army, there grow briars and thorns.

Weapons are tools of evil omen not to be used by worthy men. When they are compelled to use them, the less often, the better. Victory should not be glorified. To glorify it is to take delight in killing. Those delighted in killing cannot do what they will in the world.

The sage has no personal will; he takes the people's will as his own. He is good not only to those who are good, but also to those who are not, so all become good. He trusts not only the trustworthy, but also those who are not, so all become trustworthy.

Rule the state in an ordinary way, but fight the war in an extraodinary way. Win the world by doing nothing wrong.

Therefore, the sage says: If I do nothing wrong, the people will go the right way; if I love peace, the people will not go to war; if I do not impoverish them, they will become rich; if I have no selfish desire, they will naturally be simple.

☆

If the government is lenient, the people will be simple. If the government is severe, the people will feel a lack of freedom.

☆

Therefore the sage is fair and square without a cutting edge, thrifty but not exacting, straightforward but not haughty, bright but not dazzling.

☆

To rule people and serve heaven, nothing is better than frugality.

☆

A large state should be ruled as a small fish is cooked.

☆

No danger is greater that making light

of the foe, which may lead to the loss of my treasure. When two fighting forces are equal in strength, the wronged side will win the victory.

People do not know my words, so they do not understand me, Few people understand me, so I am still the more valuable. That is why the sage wears plain clothes, but his heart is pure as jade.

If the people fear no power, it shows that their power is great.

The people do not fear death. Why threaten them with it?

The people's starvation results from the

ruler' over-taxation, so the people starve. The people are difficult to rule, for the ruler give exacting orders, so the people are hard to rule. The people make light of their death, for the rulers overvalue their own life, so the people undervalue their death.

In accordance with the divine law, excess shall be reduced to supplement the insufficient. The human law is otherwise: man takes from the poor to give to the rich. Who could give to the world more than enough? Only the follower of the divine law.

A small state with few people may have hundreds of tools but will not use them. Its people value their life and death and will not remove far away. They may have boats and cars, but they have no need to ride. They may have armors and weapons, but they have no need to use them. They may return to the age of recording by tying knots.

In an ideal state people will find their food delicious, their clothes beautiful, their houses comfortable, and their life delightful. A neighboring state may be within sight, with cocks' crow and dogs' bark within hearing, but people will not visit each other till they die of old age.

The World and Life

☆

If more is said than done, it would be better to take the mean.

Praise and blame disturb the mind;
Fortune and misfortune affect the body.

Do your utmost to be empty-minded and hold fast to tranquillity. All things grow, I see them return to nature.

When the divine law is not followed, good and just men are needed. When the family is at odds, filial sons and kind parents are needed. When the State is at stake, loyal officials are needed.

How far away is yes from no? How far away is good from evil? What others fear, can I not fear?

The vulgar seem in the light; alone I am in the dark. The vulgar seem observant; alone I am dull.

A wanton wind cannot whisper all the morning; a sudden rain cannot howl all the day long. Who has made them so? The Heavens and the Earth. The Heavens and the Earth cannot speak long, not to speak of man.

One who sees only himself has no good sight; who thinks only himself right cannot be recognized. One who boasts of himself will not succeed; who thinks himself superior cannot be a leader.

Thus a sage is the teacher of common people, and the common people are the stuff for good men. If the teacher is not honored and the stuff not valued, even a wise man will be at a loss. This is the essential secret.

Learn to be hard as man and remain soft as woman like a stream in the world. This stream in the world will not depart from the way of virtue but rejuvenate to its infancy.

It needs observation to know others, but reflection to konw oneself. Physically strong, one can conquer others; mentally strong, one can conquer oneself. Content, one is rich; with strong will, one can persevere. Staying where one should, one can endure long; Unforgettable, one is immortal.

Therefore, a true great man prefers the thick to the thin, the substantial to the superfluous.

Thus the noble rely on the humble, and the high is based on the low.

Which do you love better, fame or life? Which do you like more, health or wealth? Which will do you more harm, gain or loss? The more you love, the more you spend. The more you store up, the more you lose. As a result, contentment brings no shame; knowledge of the limit brings no danger.

Thus you can be safe for long.

No crime is greater than insatiable desire; no woe is greater than covetous. If you know contentment comes from being content, you will always have enough.

You may know the outside world without going out. You may know the divine law without looking out of the window. The farther you go out. the less you may learn. Therefore, the sage learns all. without going far away.
He becomes well-known without looking out, and accomplishes all without doing anything.

Creation without possession, action

without interference, leadership without domination, such is the mysterious virtue.

Dull your senses and shut their doors, you need not toil all your life.
Awake your senses and satisfy them, you will be incurable all your life.

A man of high virtue may be compared to a new-born baby.

There is nothing difficult but consists of easy parts; there is no great deed but consists of small details. Therefore, the sage never tries to be great, but at last he becomes great.

A rash promise will soon be broken; much underestimation will entail much difficulty.

Make preparations before things happen; keep order before disorder sets in. A huge tree grows out of a small shoot; a nine-storied tower rises from a heap of earth; a thousand-mile journey begin with the firth step.

People engaged in a task often fail on the brink of success. If cautious from the beginning to the end, they would not have failed.

I have three treasures which I hold and keep: the first is magnanimity, the second is frugality, and the third is humility to be the last of the world.

图书在版编目（CIP）数据

千年道德经——老子：英文/徐远翔，印永健著；王壹晨，王国振译.
— 北京：五洲传播出版社，2014.6
（中国智慧）
ISBN 978-7-5085-2769-7

Ⅰ. ①千… Ⅱ. ①徐… ②印… ③王… ④王… Ⅲ. ①老子－传记－英文 Ⅳ. ①B223.15

中国版本图书馆CIP数据核字(2014)第111264号

顾　　问：	冷成金
作　　者：	徐远翔　印永健
译　　者：	王壹晨　王国振
封面绘画：	郑玉阑
插图作者：	王振国
图片提供：	CFP　东方IC　五洲传播　紫航文化
出 版 人：	荆孝敏
责任编辑：	王　莉　韩　旭
特约编辑：	王　峰
设计总监：	蔡　程
设计制作：	邹　红

千年道德经——老子

出版发行：	五洲传播出版社
地　　址：	北京市海淀区北三环中路31号生产力大楼B座7层（100088）
电　　话：	010-82005927，010-82007837（发行部）
网　　址：	www.cicc.org.cn
开　　本：	32开
印　　张：	4.5
设计承制：	北京紫航文化艺术有限公司
印　　刷：	北京盛天行健艺术印刷有限公司
版　　次：	2014年6月第一版　2014年6月第一次印刷
书　　号：	ISBN 978-7-5085-2769-7
定　　价：	53.00元